This library edition published in 2011 by Walter Foster Publishing, Inc.
Walter Foster Library
Distributed by Black Rabbit Books.
P.O. Box 3263 Mankato, Minnesota 56002

Printed in China by PRINTPLUS Limited, Shenzhen.

First Library Edition

Library of Congress Cataloging-in-Publication Data

Farrell, Russell.
  All about horses & pets / Russell Farrell and Peter Mueller. -- 1st library ed.
     p. cm.
  ISBN 978-1-936309-06-1 (hardcover)
  1. Animals in art--Juvenile literature. 2. Horses in art--Juvenile literature. 3. Drawing--Technique--Juvenile literature. I. Mueller, Peter. II. Title. III. Title: All about horses and pets.
  NC783.8.P48F37 2011
  743.6--dc22

                                                        2010004211

022010
OP1808

9 8 7 6 5 4 3 2 1

# All About
# DRAWING

## Horses & Pets

Illustrated by Russell Farrell and Peter Mueller

# Getting Started

When you **look** closely at the **drawings** in this book, you'll notice that they're made up of basic shapes, such as circles, triangles, and rectangles. To draw all your favorite animal friends, just start with simple shapes as you see here. It's easy and fun!

**Circles** are used to draw heads, chests, and hips.

# Ovals
make good profile heads and muzzles.

# Triangles
are best for angled parts, like a snake's head.

## FIND THE SHAPE!

Can you find circles, ovals, and triangles on these animals? Look closely at the dog's head and chest, and then check out the frog's body and angular legs. It's easy to see the basic shapes in any animal once you know what to look for!

# Coloring Tips

There's more than one way to bring your **horse** and **pet** pals to life on paper—you can use colored pencils, crayons, markers, or watercolor. Just be sure you have plenty of natural colors—black, brown and gray, plus yellow, orange, and red.

Colored pencil

Crayon

Pencil

Marker

Watercolor

FUN TIP!

With an assortment of horse breeds and pets to portray, the color possibilities are endless! Before you pick a coloring tool for your drawing, think about the animal's different textures. Is its skin furry, feathered, scaled, or smooth? Colored pencils have a sharp tip that is great for tiny details like small hairs and feathers. Crayons can be used to cover large areas quickly and markers make your colors appear more solid. Or try watercolor for a soft touch.

# Puppy

This **lovable** Lab is a cute pup with a **chubby** body. Begin with an oval for the tummy and a circle for the head.

5

6

# Kitten

This tiny **tabby** has a **fluffy** body and short, thick legs. Its round eyes and triangular ears look huge on its little furry frame!

5

6

Cats have excellent hearing and very flexible ears! They have 30 outer-ear muscles, which can rotate each ear a full 180 degrees. So felines can hear in all directions without moving their heads, which helps them pinpoint where sounds are coming from.

# Hanoverian Foal

Start this **long-legged** baby with two circles for the body. Then finish with a short, brushlike tail and a stiff, upright mane.

# Macaw

Use an oval to draw this **colorful, exotic** parrot's body. The bird's long feathers come to a point—so does its sharp, curved beak!

5

6

**FUN FACT**

A macaw's beak is so powerful it can easily crush a Brazil nut! And its dry, scaly tongue serves as a tool to break open and eat food.

# Australian Pony

This **sweet** little pony from "down under" has a **fine,**
delicate face and large, dark eyes. Say, "G'day, mate!"

# Hackney Horse

This handsome **show horse** is strutting its stuff—
stretch out those legs and arch that tail high!

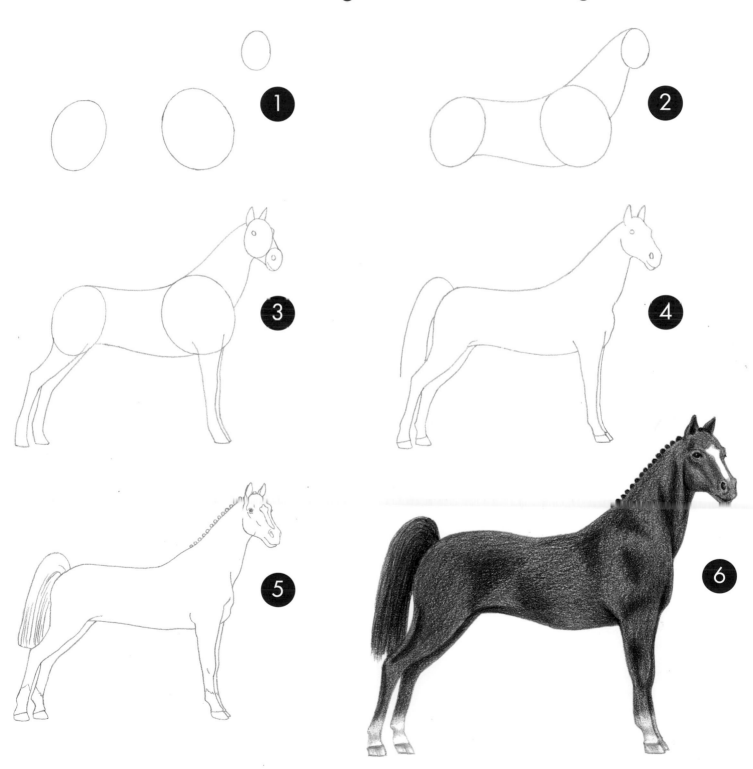

# Bunny

This **Lop-eared** rabbit's body is **round,** but it isn't a perfect circle. Its long ears droop down, but its short tail swoops up!

It's not unusual for caretakers to discover their pet bunnies fast asleep. After all, rabbits are *nocturnal,* which means they're active at night, so they sleep during the day. And, on average, rabbits take 16 naps per day to get in a full 8 hours of sleep!

4

5

6

# Frog

**green!** It isn't easy being **green!** This **amphibian** has a few unusual features, like legs that fold and eyes that sit on top of its head!

5

## FROGGY FACT

The tree frog usually keeps a low profile, blending in with the green leaves it lives on. But when threatened, it reveals its bold, red eyes and multicolored body to startle predators, before making a speedy escape.

# Pinto

This **color** breed has a **cool** patterned coat that sets it apart! A Quarter Horse or Thoroughbred Pinto can also be called a "Paint."

Both Pintos and Paints have the same patterns of coloring, so how can you tell the difference between these breeds? Every Paint is a Pinto, but not every Pinto is a Paint.

# Mouse

This **little** mammal has tiny **rodent** features: small, round eyes; a tiny pink nose; a long, thin tail; and itty, bitty toenails!

1

2

3

**4**

**5**

A mouse's front teeth keeps growing throughout its life, so it must constantly gnaw on things to wear down the teeth. This isn't hard to do, as mice will eat almost anything, from plants and insects to human food.

# Ferret

With its **slim** body and small **head,** the ferret looks similar to a cat! But its rounded ears and masked markings distinguish it from most pets.

Ferrets have been *domesticated* for even longer than cats have. Yet the approximately 8 million domestic ferrets in the United States aren't officially recognized as pets by any state government, and it's illegal to own these furry friends in the state of California!

# Percheron

The **unfeathered** Percheron is a **heavy** breed. Despite its size, it has the elegance of its Arabian ancestors.

5

6

7

# Betta

Male **fighting fish** are known for their large, colorful fins, which they proudly display when they meet another male fish!

**1**

**2**

**3**

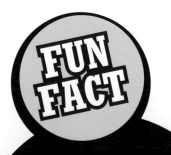

**FUN FACT**

Is there an aquarium at your dentist's office? Studies show that aquariums are relaxing and can lower the stress level of patients who are waiting for painful dental procedures.

4

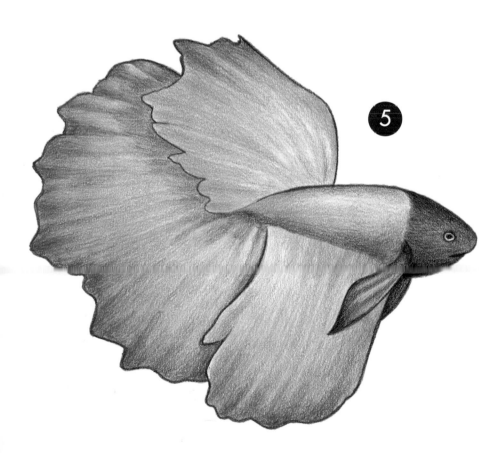

5

# FROM THE FISH FILES

Bettas are also known as Siamese fighting fish, because they are originally from the shallow waters of Thailand (formerly called Siam) and other Southeast Asian countries.

# QUICK QUIZ!

Question: Which is more colorful and has longer fins? A male Betta or a female Betta?

See the answer at the bottom of the page.

Quick Quiz Answer: A male Betta.

# American Saddlebred

This **high-spirited** horse shows off its **proud** style with a high-flying tail and a prancing step!

5

6

7

# Cockatiel

The cockatiel's **crown** of feathers **stands up** when the bird is excited, but it lies flat and curls at the end when the bird is calm.

**4**

**5**

**FUN FACT**

Because it's a social bird, your cockatiel needs a lot of attention, so the more you talk to, pet, and play with it, the better. Your cockatiel might even enjoy having a pet of its own! Experts say canaries make good pets for cockatiels. But don't expect your 'tiel to take care of the canary's feeding and clean-up; those will be your responsibilities!

# Dog

A **Rottweiler** has a thick, stocky body and a **big** head. Draw this powerful dog with strong legs, a square jaw, and a straight back.

5

IN THE DOG HOUSE

Many people incorrectly believe that the Canary Islands, located in Spain, were named after the bird. Actually, the islands were named after the Latin *Canariae insulae,* where "Canariae" refers to a large breed of dogs from Roman times. So the islands' name really means "Isle of Dogs"!

6

# Iguana

When you draw this **scaly,** sun-loving **reptile,** be sure to make its tail longer than its head and body combined!

# Shetland Pony

A **favorite** breed of pony lovers, the **adorable** Shetland is tiny but tough, with a round belly and short, stocky legs.

4

5

# Tropical Fish

# Short-Haired Cat

It's easy to **spot** this **feline's** shape because of its short coat! Start drawing this regal Bengal's body with a tall bean shape.

1

2

**FUN FACT**

The first house cats were descendants of African and European wild cats! So don't be surprised if you see a resemblance between your kitty and the big cats at the zoo.

3

4

5

6

# Parakeets

This **pair** of parakeets starts out with **similar** shapes, but the birds aren't identical. Look for the differences as you draw.

4

5

# American Quarter Horse

With its **muscular** hindquarters and **powerful** shoulders, this Western horse can sprint like an Olympian and stop on a dime!

# Morgan

**Small** but super **strong** and hardy, the Morgan has a draft horse's muscular hindquarters but thinner legs and an elegant face.

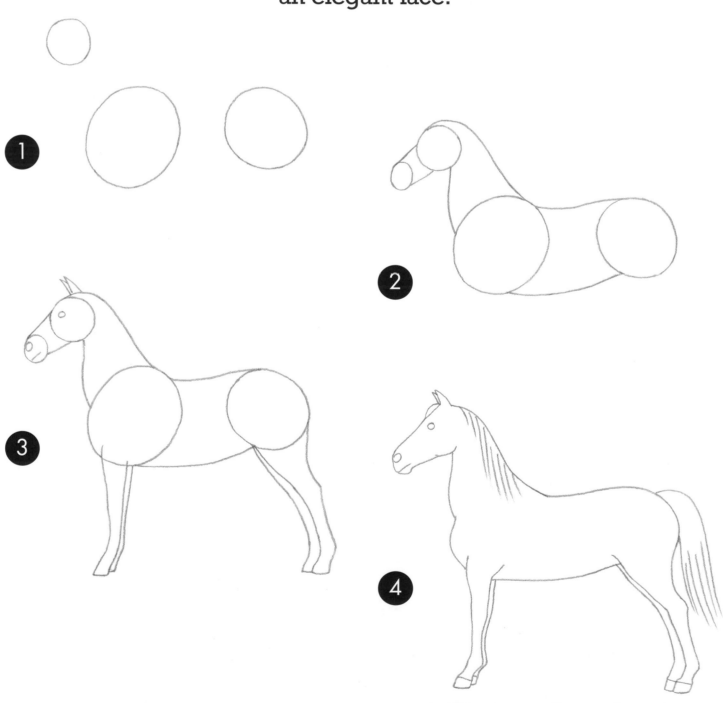

Quick Quiz Answer: True! However, it takes longer for a horse's eyes to adjust between light and dark.

5

## QUICK QUIZ!

**TRUE or FALSE?**
**A horse can see better at**
**night than a human.**

The answer is at the bottom
of the opposite page.

6

**FUN**
**FACT**

All Morgans are the descendants of the legendary Justin
Morgan horse. Originally named Figure, the colt was later
referred to by his owner's name and became famous for
his feats outperforming much larger workhorses and race-
horses. However, his finest feature was his powerful genes;
all of his offspring inherited his appearance and abilities
no matter what type of mare was bred to him!

# Goldfish

Like a game of **Go Fish,** drawing this goldfish is as simple as can be! Begin with an egg shape for the body, and then add the flowing fins!

## QUICK QUIZ!

**TRUE or FALSE?**
Fish existed even before dinosaurs roamed the earth.

The answer is at the bottom of the page.

Quick Quiz Answer: True! Some fish species were alive over 450 million years ago, whereas the first dinosaurs appeared about 200 million years later.

4

5

The most common name for pet goldfish in the United States is "Jaws." But Jaws isn't likely to respond to its name—or even remember it. The average memory span of a goldfish is only 3 seconds!

# Snake

**S-s-s-start** with two oval shapes to **snake** yourself into position to draw this slithery coiled Python.

5

**FUN FACT**

The python wraps around its prey, constricts its meal, and swallows it whole, head first. It can take up to several weeks for the python to digest a large meal, but this snake can wait a few months before its next feeding.

# Horses in Action

Whether **working** or **playing**, horses and people have been partners for thousands of years! Try your hand at drawing these active horses as they run, jump, and show off their skills!

Sliding stop

Racing

Playing polo

Jumping

Dressage

Harness racing

# Pot-Bellied Pig

**"Porkers"** like this one love to **pig** out, so it's no surprise that this swine's most recognizable feature is its big round belly.

# Friesian

Rapunzel would **envy** the long, flowing **locks** of this solid black Friesian—a heavy draft horse from the Netherlands.

# Hermit Crab

Like all **hermits,** this crab prefers to be **alone.** And there's no better place to retreat from the world than inside a shell!

Hermit crabs are nocturnal creatures, which means they are very active at night. After the sun sets, they come out in search of food, shells, and adventure. If you own hermit crabs, don't be surprised if their tank is a shambles in the morning!

5

**VERY CRABBY!**

Hermit crabs aren't terribly
friendly about sharing their space
with others. If two of these crabs
encounter one another, watch the
claws fly: The hermits will battle
it out until one falls out of
its shell.

# Appaloosa

## The **easy-going** Appaloosa is awash in **spots!**
### Along with its frosted coat pattern, it has a multi-colored tail.

**5**

The first horses in the United States arrived in 1493. By 1780, most Native American tribes had horses, including the Nez Percé of the West. Expert horsemen, the Nez Percé selectively bred spotted horses, which later became the Appaloosa breed.

**FUN FACT**

**6**

**7**

# Tarantula

An **arachnid** is a different kind of **"furry"** friend! This spider has eight shaggy legs and two shorter "arms" in front of its body.

**1**

**2**

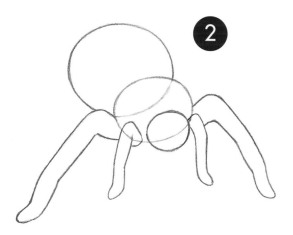

## QUICK QUIZ!

**Question: How harmful is a tarantula bite to humans?**

**The answer is at the bottom of the page.**

**3**

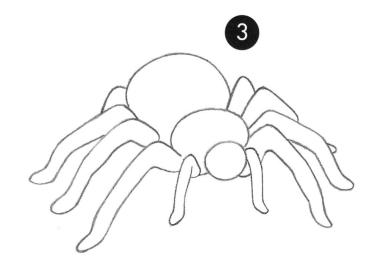

**Quick Quiz Answer: A tarantula bite is no more dangerous than a bee sting, unless a person is allergic.**

64

**FUN FACT**

Tarantulas are the only spiders that aren't able to spin webs strong enough to support their own weight.

# Highland Pony

This **sure-footed** Scottish pony has the **build** of a draft horse, with soft, silky feathers on its lower legs.

FUN FACT

Highland ponies are well adapted to
Scotland's extreme climates and can
survive outside in all weather conditions.
Their winter coat is thick and provides
plenty of insulation against the cold. Then
in the spring, they shed this layer of fur to
reveal a sleek and smooth summer coat.
These ponies are sturdy and versatile, great
for a range of activities, such as packing,
hunting, driving, jumping, and
long-distance riding.

# Tortoise

This **shell-back** moves **slowly** because it takes its home wherever it goes! Its four thick, strong legs have to work hard.

Can't tell the difference between a turtle and a tortoise? Look at their feet! A turtle spends most of its time in water and has webbed feet for swimming. A tortoise's round, stumpy feet are good for walking on land and digging burrows.

5

COOL
MOVES

Tortoises don't have teeth. They use
the sharp edges of their mouths to bite
on plants that grow low on the ground,
such as shrubs, grasses, and cactus.
Some tortoises also eat insects and
small animals. This slow-moving reptile
spends most of its day browsing for food
and slipping into cool burrows when the
sun gets too hot.

# Thoroughbred

The **fastest** breed in the world, the **athletic** and courageous Thoroughbred can run and jump for miles and miles!

# Kathiawari

This narrowly built horse from **India** has distinctive **ears** that curve inward until their tips actually touch!

**1**

**2**

**3**

**4**

**5**

## FUN FACT

This horse is small, but it's also tough, which is why the Kathiawari is a favorite of tent-pegging athletes. Originally a way to practice wild boar hunting, tent pegging is now a popular sport in India. To play the game, an athlete rides to the center of an arena and, while on horseback, uses the tip of a lance to pick up a small wooden block—or peg. Picking up the peg earns the rider half a point; picking up the peg and carrying it to the opposite corner of the arena earns a full point.

# Long-Haired Cat

Is there a **body** under that **fluff?** Of course! But for a purr-fect Persian portrait, just draw the shapes that you can see!

4

5

6

The "color point" pattern of cats like the one above is determined by heat! Color-point kittens are born light-colored because they are warm inside their mothers. After birth, the cool temperature areas (or points) of the cat darken.

# Paso Fino

Also called a "stepping" horse for its natural, lively gait, the Paso has long hind legs and pasterns and very flexible joints.

5

6

## QUICK QUIZ!

**Question: What does** *paso fino* **mean?**

**The answer is at the bottom of the opposite page.**

## FUN FACT

The Paso Fino is known for its smooth, four-beat gait that can naturally be performed since birth. Its easy, rhythmic gait provides riders with unequaled comfort, and its refined head and graceful neck give the Paso Fino a proud and stylish look.

# Guinea Pig

This little **cowlicked furball** is also called a "cavy." It may be the only pet with permanent "bedhead"!

Quick Quiz Answer: A rat. Guinea pigs are rodents.

# QUICK QUIZ!

Question: What animal is the guinea pig most closely related to: a pig, a rat, or a rabbit?

The answer is at the bottom of the opposite page.

5

FUN FACT

At birth, guinea pigs already have hair and their eyes are open. These little critters originally came from South America, where they were used for food. They are still regarded as a delicacy there today.

# Rocky Mountain Pony

Its dappled **chocolate** coloring and **creamy** mane and tail make this pretty pony a one-of-a-kind sensation!

1

2

3

4

# Glossary

**Amphibious** (AM-fib-ee-iss) - To be able to live on land and in water.

**Arachnid** (u-RACK-nid) - An insect-like creature with eight legs, such as a spider, scorpion, or tick.

**Constrict** (cun-STRICT) - To squeeze or compress.

**Crustacean** (crus-TAY-shin) - An animal that usually lives in water and has a hard outer shell and several pairs of legs.

**Domesticate** (do-MESS-ti-cayt) - To train a wild animal to live with or work for humans.

**Exoskeleton** (EK-so-ske-le-tin) - A hard, outer covering, such as the shell of a turtle, crab, or tarantula.

**Foal** (rhymes with hole) - Young horse up to one year of age.

**Gait** (GAYT) - A pattern of footsteps that a horse uses to move, such as a canter, trot, or gallop.

**Habitat** (HAB-i-tat) - Where an animal lives, such as the ocean or desert.

**Mammal** (MA-mol) - A warm-blooded animal that has hair and feeds its young milk, such as a human or dog.

**Nocturnal** (nock-TURN-ul) - If an animal is nocturnal, it means that it sleeps or hides during the day and only comes out at night.

**Predator** (PRE-da-tur) - An animal that kills and eats other animals.

**Withers** (WI-thurs) - Point at the bottom of a horse's neck from which the height of the horse is measured.